Summary of

Dr. Kellyann's
Bone Broth Diet

By Dr. Kellyann Petrucci

Smart Reads

D1527553

Note to readers:
This is an unofficial summary & analysis of Dr. Kellyann Petrucci's "Dr. Kellyann's Bone Broth Diet" designed to enrich your reading experience. The original book can be purchased on Amazon.

Download Your Free Gift

As a way to say "Thank You" for being a fan of our series, I've included a free gift for you:

Brain Health: How to Nurture and Nourish Your Brain For Top Performance

Go to www.smart-reads.com to get your FREE book.

The Smart Reads Team

Table of Contents

Overview of *Dr. Kellyann's Bone Broth Diet*

In *Dr. Kellyann's Bone Broth Diet*, Dr. Kellyann Petrucci weighs in on a more unconventional approach to losing weight, staying young, and feeling good generally. The writing is entertaining yet punctuated with the ring of truth throughout. The cookbook is user-friendly and presented an accessible yet inspirational read, which doubtless lent itself towards its success on the New York Times bestseller list. In 11 chapters, spread across three sections, the book delves into hearty subjects that range from chemical to emotional. And at the heart of it all is food and the star of the show – the Bone Broth Diet.

But the value of any cookbook is in its recipes and philosophy. The Bone Broth Diet succeeds on both fronts. First, it offers several effective and accessible avenues towards weight loss. And secondly, doubling down, she does not at any point underestimate her audience. Every anecdote conveys the experience of the everyday person with normal and natural reservations. That level of being able to connect to the Bone Broth Diet is essential. Every recipe ingests the heart and soul that this writer has infused in her work. And this diet does not exist in a vacuum. These components have already become massively popular throughout the United States, and in a sense, this writer merely offers her professional and artistic take on them.

But beyond the optimism, the Bone Broth Diet offers results. Countless people utilize this dietary path today, and it has much to do with its effectiveness as both a food and dietary regimen. If you are intrigued about the concept of losing weight but experience that twitch of hesitation when the thought crosses your sitting mind, read this book. It may deliver the spark you need to find some peace, structure, and weight loss in your life. As one of many successful books in her catalog, Kellyann Petrucci hits it out of the park with the Bone Broth Diet. Even those who are skeptical of the diet will no doubt never think of broth the same. And perhaps that is for the better.

Chapter One

Chapter one is entitled My 21-Day Challenge To You: Lose the Weight – and the Wrinkles. It sets the tone for the book amicably, as Dr. Kellyann Petrucci introduces herself, and then the reader to the object of this read through an anecdote in New York City. Here, she shares her discovery of bone broth mania. An obsession with the stuff has exploded popularly from health enthusiasts – so much that the substance rivals Starbucks. The writer describes it as a commodity that sells faster than the high-end chefs can produce it. But though the focus is on food, it is led by a strong undercurrent of her fresh yet refined perspective on health and food. More specifically, she wields a deep knowledge of the latest city and nationwide diets and how food and culture intertwine. The adventure begins.

Next, with style, Dr. Kellyann demonstrates that she has been living and leading ahead of the curve with this ingenious concoction, which she describes as more than food. Bone broth, according to her, is concentrated healing. And this conceptualization sticks. The language she uses to articulate this function is idyllic, painting a picture of nourishment, conjuring memories of warm stomachs filled with broth and comfort. Kellyann then delivers the staggering statement that will have you hooked with intrigue: stick to this diet for 21 days, and you will see the results. Petrucci claims that the soup not only helps you lose weight but also takes years off your life. How does she expect to back up that statement, you might wonder? Dr. Kellyann is not called such for no reason. She explains her certifications as a certified nutritional consultant with 20 years of experience working with a host of different people. And her perspective is demonstrative of this.

And through her prose, she demonstrates her passion, which makes thumbing through this cookbook entertaining and in a rhythm. Her writing clarifies that her talent lies in transforming people. With hundreds of people that Kellyann has directly helped over the years and the millions indirectly, it is difficult to argue with her goal without looking at the numbers. Every one of her clients has had firsthand experience with the power of bone broth, and often, it brought out the real possibilities of transformation regarding weight and looking and feeling young.

Then the doctor proceeds by citing an anecdote about someone she calls Jenny. She is a client who, from the outset, was determined that Kellyann could not help her lose weight. And we learn that this stems from a fear of dying from diabetes - a sobering reminder that losing weight can derive from existential anxiety or unsorted trauma. She goes through how Jenny developed a toxic relationship around food that reflected her unfolding life. And this snapshot into the human condition demonstrates how bad habits are the most difficult to unlearn. But fortunately, her client succeeded in her attempts and found peace of mind. The success happened thanks to Dr. Kellyann's passive yet time-tested approach. She did not push Jenny to do anything, nor did she promise anything. The aspect spoke for itself, and in this sense, it was attraction, not promotion, that stuck with the client in the end.

Next, Kellyann dives into the more technical and tangible aspects of the diet and transformative process. With provocative titles like My Secret Weapon For Fast, Hunger-Free Weight Loss: Bone Broth, one cannot help but read the finer details and stay for the stories of personal growth. Bone broth lacks carbs and calories, enabling someone who is fasting to have as much as they want during that process. It fills you up yet does not weigh you down, as it were. Furthermore, the liquid gold contains significant amounts of collagen, which act as an anti-aging agent, as the collagen zaps the wrinkles. But that is not all. Bone broth detoxifies your body, heals your gut, heals your joints, and is anti-inflammatory.

She then breaks down the differences between acute and chronic inflammation and how, ultimately, foods that decrease inflammation will help you lose weight. It is a strong indicator that the concept of inflammation will echo throughout the rest of the book. Specifically, the power of anti-inflammatory foods has to do with insulin resistance and how the body reacts to metabolic changes. The combined power of fasting plus bone-broth is doubly effective, and for those who are already considering that path, it is an added benefit of doing so. Next, Petrucci dives into the foods that will help you burn fat – because, after all, fasting does include periods of eating substantively. She writes with plenty of reassuring and logical calls to action. Lastly, Dr. Kellyann concludes this chapter by stating that all she needs is three weeks and then explains why.

Chapter Two

The second chapter is entitled The Basics of the Bone Broth Diet. Here, Kellyann Petrucci gives a well-thought-out overview of non-conforming weight loss methodologies. She confronts the skepticism and natural hesitancy with another anecdote. This time, her story addresses the stigma against dieting. The person whom that anecdote recalls is Charlie, a 30-year-old soccer player who has now developed a beer belly. Beer bellies, as you may know, represent that source of frustration or anxiety for many men. Right away, the anecdote asserts its appeal to all genders. The beer belly is universal. Initially, Charlie operated under the assumption that dieting is nothing more than counting calories, but he soon was pleasantly surprised.

Another stigma that the doctor directly addresses and transcends is that dieting consists of eating dry and tasteless foods. Petrucci does not want you to count calories or eat such misery-inducing substances. Instead, she wants you to live it up and make the minimum sacrifices for the maximum effect. That is why bone broth stands in stark contrast to those bleaker realities, as it represents a legit alternative to the idea that one must suffer to succeed. The concept of eating as much broth as you want is infinitely more appealing than letting the mind wander about going without food. And the other half of the beauty lies in non-fasting days. For the other five days of the week, you allow yourself the freedom, which was never stripped away, of eating three meals and two snacks per day.

But it is vital to recognize that, ultimately, if all else fails, you should eat when faced with irreconcilable discomfort or pain that stems from the diet. If the diet is unmanageable for you, there is no such failure in breaking or bending it. First, it is not realistic to assume that you can stick to a static change in such clear and defined terms. There will be times where you will stray from this path, and the doctor knows this firsthand through her experience in the field. There are plenty of external factors which may add unforeseeable stress in our lives. That makes balancing a diet amid those circumstances incredibly difficult, seemingly impossibly so. And there is a valid psychological reason for not equating eating with failure. That is because over-focusing on failures can breed resentment, discouragement, and giving up entirely. Allow yourself that grey area of making a few mistakes along the way, as it can take a lot of weight off your shoulders and could be what makes a diet stick in your life for once. Here, the doctor will teach you to do just that, to take that negative and make it into a positive.

Another reason why you should not stress in the name of your diet is you may be addicted to certain foods, and this zero-tolerance approach likely will not help matters. Thus, recognizing that many people are in some way addicted to such things as caffeine, not to mention items such as cigarettes, alcohol, etc. Acknowledging the addictions that come with food in the modern age can allow you to be more realistic with what you face. How often do you drink coffee or soda, for example? Or how often do you eat candy? Asking yourselves these questions at the beginning is a must.

For those with varying addictions to food, there is not a one-size-fits-all approach to the issue. You can wean yourself off instead of giving up everything simultaneously, for example. And this more nuanced, more compassionate approach lends itself towards a more accessible effort. In turn, more people should feel empowered to try to lose weight and not be afraid of making mistakes. There is the other side, though, wherein constantly trying a diet to no avail can be brutal. Dr. Kellyann considers this, fortunately. And the fact that she is making a point of addressing the overarching concerns of the average person is profoundly refreshing.

The following section explores whether the Bone Broth Diet is the right choice for you. She begins by addressing pregnancy. If you are pregnant, she says, do not try this diet. While that makes sense from the outset, it is vital to heed her words in context. Next, she addresses diabetes. Even though folks with diabetes can benefit from this diet, it can also lower your blood sugar.

So, if any at-risk folks wish to try this diet, then their doctors will have to monitor fasting efforts incredibly closely to detect any signs of dangerous hypoglycemia. You should only start a diet of this nature if your doctor is on board. Dr. Kellyann then goes into myriad other illnesses and medical contexts in which you should explore a professional opinion before proceeding with her diet. All readers should read this section carefully if they are considering following suit. She concludes with the length of the program (three weeks), the results one might expect, and the erasure of wrinkles before more thoroughly breaking down the diet by each day and possible emotions you may experience along the way.

Chapter Three

The next chapter is entitled, *Your Mini-Fasting Secret to Success: Liquid Gold.* It begins with Dr. Kellyann addressing what she effectively refers to as mini fasts, which you will take twice per week, should you choose to take this bone broth route. While she acknowledges the credibility of several diets that take massive amounts of time – as most often do – Kellyann goes into the nitty-gritty of why mini fasting is an impressive short-term solution. She returns to the more human side of things, acknowledging that most of humanity is opposed to new things, like sweeping dietary changes. But the writer understands these concerns, and if any diet could transcend those instincts, it is sure to be this one.

Next, Dr. Kellyann does an impressive job conveying the subtle complexities of bone broth. She effectively demonstrates its tasteful palette and its time-tested role in weight transformation. The doctor makes the combination sound appetizing. And she clarifies through anecdotes and research that it is indeed possible to incorporate these changes to positive results. Moreover, the informative passages introduce several robust dietary options that the average person could try to tangible measures of success. And the fact that her clients have been impressed speaks volumes to the power of such unconventional dietary methodologies. When she sees her clients again after three weeks, they have lost 15 pounds, and their skin looks healthier.

There is much to unpackage here, and admittedly the results are limited on her experiences. Still, perhaps the most central indicator of the Bone Broth Diet and its success is the way her clients felt after only twenty-one days. Fortunately, and to the surprise of many skeptics, they felt great! Not only did bone broth work for them, but they also enjoyed eating it – something they would have sworn was impossible at the start. This inspirational anecdote demonstrates the effectiveness of this specific diet among the overall joy one can attain by trying something new. And when something new works, the joy multiplies and becomes intensified. This measure of success is something that anyone can strive for.

This segues to the next section, wherein Dr. Kellyann explains bone broth as the original fast food. That is because it only takes about five minutes to throw the ingredients together, although the product sits for hours on a slow cooker or stove. And it is an ancient culinary method, with roots that go back hundreds of years. An interesting moment occurs here, where the quickness of cooking bone broth is juxtaposed by the fact that it is also incredibly slow to cook. You cannot rush perfection, naysayers.

Plus, those interested in the many wonders of bone broth have more to discover. The broth carries the added benefit of enriching your home with warm, engaging smells – an aromatherapy process you were not aware of beginning. The more you cook the bone broth ingredients, the healthier the bone broth becomes, and the richer those healing scents become. In this sense, cooking bone broth can detoxify your home in several ways. The bones melt away and release nutrients that speak to our bodies chemically in a way that other foods cannot. Thus, bone broth is uniquely tasty for both the mouth and the cells. And its healing effects on the nose and spirit are nothing to skip over, either.

Next, Kellyann goes deeper into the benefits of bone broth by speaking towards its more technical components. More specifically, it contains collagen and gelatin. And Kellyann goes into great depth about these two chemicals. She explains how they help fight wrinkles and keep your skin looking young. First, understand that collagen comes from the bone and is high in amino acids. Second, as the collagen cooks, that collagen becomes gelatin over time. Additionally, gelatin heals more than only your skin: it heals your gut and fights inflammation. Her patients who experience arthritis or celiac disease swear by the Bone Broth Diet, and it is easy to see why. And because of these healing agents found within the bone, you will want to spend a thoughtful amount of time searching and securing the best bones. But she will touch on that in more depth as the book develops.

Continuing, Dr. Kellyann further explores the nutritional content of bone broth. If you began this book with zero knowledge about this food, you could surely finish it with a swath of relevant information. The writer visits how liquid gold offers several vitamins, minerals, fats, and alkylglycerols. All this goes to help your body in neat, specific ways. Specifically, bone broth recharges and replenishes your body by keeping your hormones in balance, energizing your cells, and enhancing your digestion. But bone broth also helps repair joints – a service that many of us growing older could use. The ramifications of this could be far-reaching, as a new approach to healing could ensue. We will have to wait and see if the world catches on.

But let us return to cartilage. It is highly present in bone broth, as well, which contains glucosamine and chondroitin sulfate. If you are unsure what those chemicals are, just know that these two supplements are what many doctors prescribe to various patients to keep their joints in good form. She then cites a 2015 study wherein those two ingredients showed to help prevent lung cancer. How? It all comes back to fighting inflammation, as it not only impedes the body's ability to regulate itself but also affects how you perceive your progress.

The following section is entitled *Glycine And Other Key Amino Acids.* Here, the fearless writer dissects the differences between conditional and essential amino acids. Specifically, bone broth is high in amino acids, and these are referred to as conditional amino acids because the body is assumed to produce enough of them naturally. But Dr. Petrucci takes issue with this long-held assumption by pointing to the modern world, which so often deprives common folk of the health and longevity they deserve. As a result, the writer offers four vital conditional amino acids that could greatly help you. Fortunately, all four are found directly in bone broth. They are glycine, proline, arginine, and glutamine. She then breaks down some more advantages of mini-fasting from a technical standpoint, exploring concepts like BDNF (brain-derived neurotrophic factor) and HGH (human growth hormone). The chapter concludes but the adventure ensues.

Chapter Four

Chapter four is entitled *Metabolic Magic for Your Non-fasting Days*. The first section explicitly deals with foods that melt off fat and erase wrinkles. So, if that is what you came for, then you can rest assured that you will not be disappointed. But assuming Dr. Kellyann already has convinced you to take a journey of mini fasting and to continue reading, then now it is time to explore what occurs on the remaining five non-fasting days of the week. She warns that you will feel like you are betraying your diet, but you are not. It will take your mind some time and energy to adjust to that fact. Instead, you will feel like you are enjoying the high life, as it were. It is still important to not lose track of the larger goals, however. Still, she has concocted three weeks of meals for you to enjoy and look forward to and she believes in you, readers. And this alone should motivate even the most skeptical of the bunch.

Next, the book explores with intrigue several recipes that have been carefully assembled and translated onto the page. And these recipes that Dr. Kellyann has created adapt to the various needs and skill levels of all cooks out there – a fact that makes the Bone Broth Diet seem more accessible and delectable by each turn of the page. What is more, these foods are high in blasting away fat and making that face look youthful. And if you are skeptical at the outset, you will be pleasantly surprised upon reading through the delicious recipe options awaiting you. That's right – the food is genuinely tasty, and so you have something to look forward to during those moments when everything may feel overwhelming. Just remember that you can treat yourself to the high-life and still work towards your goals of weight loss and anti-aging.

But first, Dr. Petrucci does the necessary task of eliminating foods that are antithetical to the entire premise of this diet. After all, you cannot assume to eat whatever you want with no repercussions regarding the diet. But first, she connects using compassion and softens the blow. Kellyann acknowledges it may not be the most appealing thing in the world, to cut out a bunch of otherwise tasty foods. The list of foods to avoid is a bit long, and it will hurt a little reading it. But she knows her clientele – and this should inspire you. Because if other regular people can stick to the diet, so can you. Plus, she says, once you dive into some of the great foods you will be preparing over the coming weeks, you will still happily enjoy eating without the nagging thought of the diet. And the point, after all, is to transform your body into a well-oiled fat-burning machine and your mind into a beacon of peace and motivation. By reading ahead, you will continue your metamorphosis.

To begin, she discusses a few factors in great depth. First, she addresses the switch you must flip within, the one that will turn your body on to burning fat instead of burning sugar. This is triggered by the dietary choices you will incorporate into your daily routine. Even though this will confuse your body, it will be for a good cause, as this will enable the invaluable process of ketosis. Ketosis, she says, is the biggest secret to amplifying and accelerating your weight loss. Shout out to ketones. That is because ketosis deals with dormant fat by extracting and burning it during this process. This shortcut is something most readers will come back to over and over, digesting as much information as possible. Get ready for ketosis, folks.

Another thing you must accomplish to trigger this critical component of the Bone Broth Diet is to mitigate inflammation. The doctor cites a statistic and posits there is a positive relationship between obesity and inflammatory disease, which will give most readers pause. You will likely respond by interrogating whether you find yourself in a similar position. Some will schedule an appointment with the doctor immediately. Maybe that is for the best. But whether you face the possibility of incurring that disease or merely wish to lose a little pudge, tackling inflammation is a must. And it is a good thing that the Bone Broth Diet specifically centralizes inflammation as the main villain in this story. Tackling inflammation in an effective way will do great things for your skin and how you feel generally. Also, it will heal your gut, undoing the damage that has amassed over your eating career. That is where specific foods that damage your innards must be cast aside and left uneaten. If this feels discouraging, just remember to keep focused on the end goal and the fact that it is only for twenty-one days. At every turn, this diet is meant to inspire and reassure, not to discourage or destabilize your senses.

Then, there is a long list of everything that must go. Some readers may want to take a deep breath before reading. It is a tough pill to swallow, and this will doubtless be one of the more challenging aspects of the entire reading experience. Some of the more unexpected choices include bread, pasta, and various cooking oils. For most people, that bubble has burst. Cutting out sugary foods is obvious, but the writer insists that this may help beyond weight loss. Instead, cutting out sugary foods could be a preventative action against pancreatic cancer, and cancer is a strong enough motivating factor currently.

She then lists the many names that sugar goes by. The countless iterations and nicknames can be tough to keep up with or memorize, so it is helpful that the writer includes an easy-to-follow list in the book that readers can revisit at their leisure. That can help readers spot the foods they must be vigilant in cutting out and applying it to their eating experiences. She warns again that sugar is addictive and withdrawals are real. So, if you have a true dependency on sugary foods and substances, you can expect some hardships and resistance from your body. Additionally, artificial sweeteners, grains, dairy, soy, oils, beans and potatoes, artificial ingredients, alcohol – they must all go! Now, take a deep breath.

Next comes all the food that you can eat. After reading, you can immediately celebrate. But before Dr. Kellyann identifies these sanctuaries for you, she insists you will remain excited and satisfied throughout your meals and explains the logic behind her reasonings. For one, these foods are low in carbs and are lipotropic. For another, they nourish skin with healthy fats, detox your cells, regulate your hormones, and mitigate inflammation. She then doubles down with an anecdote to show through lived experience how this plays out on an average person. This time the client's name is Merris, and the experience she draws upon here is clearly one of Dr. Kellyann's favorites. The writer then lists several examples of meats, fish, eggs, veggies, fruits, healthy fats, shakes, fermented foods, condiments, flours, and beverages you may consume on your five non-fasting days, adding context and tips along the way.

The remaining sections intend to get you mentally segued into this diet. First, Dr. Kellyann conveys how important it is to drink lots of water on your off days. If you are not already in the habit of staying hydrated, become acclimated. Second, the doctor talks about portions and shares helpful tips about portion sizing. Following that, she shares her meal plan for each day and offers several troubleshooting tips. She argues you will not believe how satisfied you become from only bone broth and these limited yet somehow vast culinary options at your feet.

Chapter Five

This chapter marks the beginning of the second section, concerned with recipes, meal plans, and batch-cooking tips. Here, the writer explores nine recipes for broth, assuming you do not already own a mass quantity of the stuff. She recommends trying out several recipes to keep your taste on its feet, as well as to provide a wide array of nutrients to your body. She begins by discussing the bones that will sit at the forefront of your broth. Readers should, if possible, get these from organic, grass-fed, pasture-raised animals because they offer more nutrient density and fewer toxins. Additionally, the writer explores bone broth – and it is, admittedly, not rocket science. However, Dr. Kellyann insists newcomers should be aware of a few things before they get to cooking.

First, the cooked broth becomes like gelatin when you cool it, and if it is not, you should consider if you selected the right bones, if you used too much water, if you boiled the broth (you should not), and if you overcooked or undercooked the broth. She singles out vinegar specifically, arguing that the stuff dissolves the boners, releasing the maximum of specific nutrients that will help get all this transformative work started. But do not worry about it overpowering your broth. After cooking, you will not even taste it.

Then, after you have the basics down, you should experiment at your leisure, as you may discover some great combinations and iterations. The first ingredient Dr. Kellyann recommends is thyme, as it pairs well with chicken and turkey broths, followed by garlic. And she also reminds readers that they can always experiment on a smaller scale by testing these combinations in a cup. She then gives some additional preparation tips before diving into the recipes.

The first four recipes that the doctor shares include those for chicken, beef, and fishbone broth.

Then she offers five more recipes, a bit more elaborate – including Thanksgiving turkey bone broth, Asian chicken bone broth, Eastern European beef bone broth, French onion beef bone broth, and Italian beef bone broth. Next, she delves into 16 different potential snacks for you to eat at 7:00 pm. When preparing each snack, it is essential to portion correctly. These snacks include smoked salmon, cooked chicken breast, turkey or chicken wrapped in lettuce, beef or bison topped with salsa, pot roast, scrambled eggs, baked scotch egg, egg drop soup, turkey meatloaf, turkey breast, salad greens, baked or broiled whitefish, boiled or steamed shrimp, turkey chili, and approved shakes.

Chapter Six

This chapter is concerned with entrees that blast fat and soups that are beneficial on non-fasting days. Dieting and fine dining go hand in hand. Taboo foods like beef, avocados, eggs, clarified butter, and coconut oils are all on the table because they dramatically decrease your insulin levels in addition to a host of other ideal ramifications. These foods will make you lose weight, which is surprising given how delectable it all tastes. Not only do they reduce insulin, but they also detoxify your gut, mitigate and reverse inflammation, burn off pounds, and make your skin look younger.

Next, Dr. Kellyann explores how to make use of this diet without cooking frequently. Because although the Bone Broth Diet is conducive for any cooking skill level, some people merely do not have the time it takes. And who can blame them? That is why this writer suggests going to a supermarket and fixing yourself a bowl, under specific limitations, of salad. Or get a bag of frozen vegetables and steam them on the stovetop.

She then suggests loading up on blueberries. Blueberries are easy to eat and are incredibly healthy for you. So, do not worry if you eat a ton of them. And although you should not feel bad about eating any frozen veggies, the ideal vegetables to use are those that are fresh. She then shares how to make a memorable salad as an entrée. The advice includes choosing protein you enjoy, selecting greens for crispiness, adding veggies for crunchiness, and using salad dressing for flavor and healthy fat. With protein, you should eat what you want because it is worth it and filling. Additionally, purchase rotisserie chicken that has no additives. Buy extra virgin olive oils and vinegar to produce a custom dressing on the fly. And if you are specific when you order, it is possible to eat out and stick to a diet.

Next, Dr. Kellyann explores the options for readers who love to cook, including several genuinely hearty breakfasts and gourmet meals. It is more than possible to stick within the boundaries on your off days. The writer also stresses the importance of clarified butter and explains how to make and preserve it. Next, she lists fourteen delicious breakfast foods to enjoy. That includes 1) asparagus-and-mushroom crustless quiche, 2) baked egg cups with spinach, 3) baked scotch eggs, 4) beef, egg, and mushroom breakfast, 5) chili omelet, 6) egg-and-tomato skillet, 7) Mediterranean scramble, 8) pork and eggs, 9) sausage-and-apple frittata, 10) smoked salmon and eggs, 11) southwest breakfast scramble, 12) vegetable frittata, 13) zucchini breakfast cakes, and lastly, 14) breakfast egg muffins with Italian sausage.

Next, Dr. Kellyann explores lunch and dinner entrée options. First, she selects 21 chicken or turkey entrees. That includes 1) Asian turkey burgers, 2) turkey taco salad, 3) kale salad with turkey, 4) turkey meatloaf loaded with vegetables, 5) rich and hearty turkey chili, 6) middle eastern meatballs, 7) easy turkey burgers, 8) easy roast turkey breast, 9) turkey or chicken chorizo, 10) turkey-or-chicken Italian sausage, 11) turkey-or-chicken savory sausage, 12) one-skillet zucchini pasta with sausage, 13) orange-rosemary chicken salad, 14) chicken salad with crunch, 15) braised chicken with leeks and mushrooms, 16) chicken stir-fry, 17) chopped balsamic chicken salad, 18) chicken with orange-rosemary sauce, 19) easy roast chicken, 20) easy roast chicken breasts, and 21) creamy chicken curry.

Next, Dr. Kellyann discusses four lunch and dinner entrees composed of beef and bison. That includes Greek-style beef or bison burgers, fiesta beef fajitas, easy pot roast, and easy beef or bison burgers. Following are two pork lunch and dinner options, including 1) pork tenderloin with apples and onions and 2) balsamic roast pork loin. After, she examines four fish lunch and dinner options, including tuna-stuffed tomatoes, salmon patties, seared scallops, and roasted salmon gremolata.

In the following section, the writer addresses grab-and-go meals. That includes turkey meatloaf, eggs and salmon, chicken, egg drop soup, turkey chili, instant salad, bone broth soup, turkey breast, tuna or salmon, burgers, and beef fajita lettuce wraps. She then shares a thoughtful section filled with cooking tips and preparation instructions. She begins with eleven entrée soups, including 1) Tuscan seafood soup, 2) tomato, basil, and Italian sausage soup, 3) South of the border chicken soup, 4) bone-broth egg-drop soup, 5) Portuguese kale and sweet potato soup, 6) Italian wedding soup, 7) herb-infused chicken soup, 8) hearty beef-and-vegetable soup, 9) Greek-style lemony chicken soup, 10) cream of wild mushroom soup, and 11) coconut curried chicken soup. Following are six call-to-action soup options, including 1) salmon-and-leek chowder, 2) watercress soup, 3) cool and creamy avocado-pumpkin soup, 4) red bell pepper soup, 5) shiitake mushroom soup and 6) Mary's hot and sour soup.

Chapter Seven

Chapter seven is entitled *Luscious Sides, Condiments, and "Extras" For Your Non-Fasting Days.* At this point, Dr. Kellyann has shared dozens of recipes and options that can either strictly guide you or inspire you to concoct your meals based on a few central components. These include vegetable side dishes, condiments, salad dressings, shakes, and desserts. Plus, there are certain gelatins you should strive to replicate because they are effective at zapping wrinkles. Then, ten low-carb veggie options. These include 1) Mediterranean potato salad, 2) zucchini wide-cut pasta, 3) ratatouille, 4) roasted portobello burger buns 5) roasted sweet onions, 6) coasted curry cauliflower, 7) napa slaw creamy ginger dressing, 8) lemony cucumber salad, 9) lemon-roasted asparagus, 10) garlic mashed cauliflower potatoes, and 11) cauliflower rice.

Next, Dr. Kellyann explores four starchy vegetables: baked or mashed sweet potatoes, oven-steamed winter squash, roasted winter squash, and sweet-and-spicy roasted sweet potatoes. Following that, she discusses salad dressings and condiments, including spicy 1) lime vinaigrette, 2) balsamic vinaigrette, 3) creamy avocado sauce or salad dressing (three variations), 4) creamy ginger dressing, 5) French vinaigrette, 6) lemon vinaigrette or dressing, 7) orange vinaigrette or creamy orange dressing, 8) cocktail sauce, 9) marinara sauce, 10) homemade mayonnaise and six variations, 11) ketchup, 12) roasted garlic, 13) fiesta marinade, 14) Kellyann's favorite marinade, 15) creamy chimichurri, 16) pesto, 17) Pico de Gallo, 18) roasted red pepper sauce, 19) roasted salsa Verde, 20) Santa Fe sauce, and 21) smoky chipotle salsa.

In the next section, Dr. Kellyann discusses desserts, including baked apples, poached pears, and strawberries, with a balsamic reduction. Next, she explores shakes. These include baked apple shake, green goddess shake, strawberry shake, blue and green shake. Next, she recommends recipes that feature gelatin, including sweet black cherry gummies, panna cotta with balsamic-soaked strawberries, salmon mousse, gazpacho molded salad, chicken pate, and mushroom pate.

Chapter Eight

This chapter is entitled *Making It Easy*, and it is easy to see why. Dr. Kellyann addresses from the outset the reality of dieting on such stuff as bone broth. It is more complex than dieting on tasteless, frozen, assembled foods delivered to your door. Ultimately, real food trumps lifeless consumption. That is why the topic of meal plans is vital. And it is why Dr. Kellyann shares some invaluable tips for batch cooking. Here, she examines three weeks of meal plans, breaking down each day with its contents spotlighted for your reading digestion. Not only does this make your meal a bit more fun, but it also makes each meal that much easier. There is no need to add to the stress on your plate.

The first meal plan features five unique meals. Day one consists of baked scotch eggs for breakfast, a turkey meatloaf loaded with vegetables with ketchup for lunch, and easy roast chicken breasts for dinner. Day two consists of baked egg cups with spinach for breakfast, easy roast chicken breast leftovers for lunch, and rich and hearty turkey chili. Day three consists of baked scotch eggs for breakfast, turkey taco salad for lunch, and a Greek-style bison or beef burger for dinner. Day four consists of baked egg cups with spinach for breakfast, turkey meatloaf for lunch, and chicken with orange rosemary sauce for your dinner. Finally, day five consists of southwest breakfast scramble for breakfast, orange chicken salad for lunch, and roasted salad gremolata for dinner.

The meal plan for week two is as follows. On day one, Mediterranean scramble for breakfast, kale salad with turkey for lunch, and balsamic roast pork loin for dinner. On day two, pork and eggs for breakfast, tuna-stuffed tomato for lunch, and sliced turkey breast for dinner. On day three, vegetable frittata for breakfast, chopped balsamic chicken salad for lunch, and stir-fry for dinner. On day four, smoked salmon and eggs for breakfast, fiesta beef fajitas for lunch, and one-skillet zucchini pasta with sausage for dinner.

For week three, the meal plans are as follows. Day one features sausage-and-apple frittata for breakfast, one-skillet zucchini pasta with sausage for lunch, and braised chicken with leeks and mushrooms for dinner. Day two features zucchini breakfast cakes for breakfast, chicken salad with crunch for lunch, and creamy chicken curry for dinner. Day three includes sausage with apple frittata for breakfast, curried chicken for lunch, and an Asian turkey burger for dinner. Day four features zucchini breakfast cakes for breakfast, an Asian turkey burger for lunch, and salmon Gremolata for dinner. Day five includes beef, egg, and mushroom breakfast, one roasted or grilled chicken breast for lunch, and easy beef or bison burger for dinner.

Next, Dr. Kellyann explains ingredients you will want to stock up on before dieting. These include proteins, fats, vegetables, fruits, seasonings, spices, and canned, jarred, or bottled goods. Next are some in-depth tips for batch cooking, the best way to prepare for the inevitable craziness of life that impedes your free time and energy to whip up something akin to your diet, which is also easy. She wants you to know that you can make a ton of great foods at one time to maximize your batches and slash your cooking time. Some easy meals to cook in batches include turkey or chicken Italian sausage, easy roast chicken breasts, rich and hearty turkey chili, easy roast chicken, and easy beef or bison burgers. But before you start cooking, make sure to set up all your ingredients, as this will make it easier for you when the time comes.

Next, Dr. Kellyann delves into how to batch prepare your vegetables for the upcoming week. The easiest way to do this, she claims, is to wash a variety of veggies at one time and pack them away into tightly sealed containers or resealable bags. Essentially, you should rinse and cut as many as possible to ensure that your veggies are ready to go for various uses throughout the week. Additionally, while you are batch prepping your vegetables for the week, be sure to batch cook your bone broth as well. After all, that liquid gold is the crux of this entire diet. Plus, it is effortless to throw the bones, vegetables, and seasonings in the pot to cook for hours. Do it in minutes for a week of rewards.

Chapter Nine

Chapter nine is entitled *Add More Fat-Burning Power With Exercise*, and it marks the third and final section of the book, which is concerned with exercise, stress reduction, and a slim mindset. The first trick that Dr. Kellyann explores fearlessly is exercise. Yes, she realizes you may have your reservations about it, but exercise is the ideal supplement to take in addition to the diet – especially this one. It keeps you in slender form, helps you feel better, and lowers your risk of developing cancer – all while costing nothing. Exercise is the supplement to take along with the Bone Broth Diet because it helps you lose weight faster.

Moreover, after dieting, and more specifically when you are no longer mini-fasting, exercising will be how you can keep the weight off. It will become your new status quo, and so it is vital to dive in and know everything there is to know about exercise. The fact that exercise can help cure depression is one of its great, year-round benefits. The doctor then cites a statistic to make the case that often, folks who exercise tend to fight off more diseases as they get older. And one of the takeaways is exercise does not have to be taxing. Even simple physical activities such as walking can have profound benefits in slimming you and keeping you young. That is why Dr. Kellyann makes it a point to carve out a specific walking program for the Bone Broth Diet. Because even walking for half the week will add to your weight loss over these three weeks.

More broadly, exercise transforms your body and mind. Here, Dr. Kellyann introduces her concept of primal rules. First, exercise turns your body into a natural fat burner, enabling you to lose weight faster and while sitting and being inactive. Second, exercise fights depression through biochemistry. Endorphins naturally make you feel good, and fortunately, exercising releases a lot of them. Additionally, exercise helps break down kynurenine, which effectively helps break down depression organically. And third, it makes you generally healthy overall by lowering blood glucose levels, reducing belly fat, increasing circulation, preventing heart disease, and reducing the risk of certain cancers.

Next, the doctor recognizes that one can get slim without any exercise. That will doubtless come as a pleasant surprise for those looking to exhaust as little physical fuel as possible. Come now! You will lose more weight by adding exercise to your daily routine no matter how busy you are. And is that not the intention of the diet in the first place? That is why Dr. Kellyann provides four simple yet timelessly extensive exercise paths for newcomers to the Bone Broth Diet. That array of diversity will be necessary given no patient can likely stick to a singular exercise plan. People need options, after all. Thankfully, she has them laid out for your reading comprehension. That is also important because different people want different things out of their diet. Some want to lose more weight than others, and so on.

Instead of submitting a one-size-fits-all prescription for exercise, Dr. Kellyann suggests the following four plans to experiment with at your thoughtful discretion. Option one is entitled Easy Does It, and it is for those who struggle with even the easy exercises. Get an activity tracker or cheap pedometer, and on each non-fasting day, walk ten thousand steps. If you are ready for more, move on to option two, entitled Kathy Smith's Special Workout – Just for You. This option speaks to the talents of Kellyann's friend, a bestselling New York Times author in her own right, with three decades of field experience. The method relies heavily on periodization, which essentially refers to varying your exercises across lines of length, activity, and intensity. The third option is to keep up with your regular workouts. If you already go to the gym, likely you are already on the right track.

But do not push yourself too hard. After all, this is not only bad for you, but it is unnecessary as you will lose weight regardless. The last option is to do what you love. After all, life is not worth living any other way. Any exercise that you genuinely enjoy doing is worth exploring because it will make losing weight and sticking to the ambitious diet that much easier.

Chapter Ten

The second chapter of this third and final section of the book is entitled Get Slimmer By Lowering Your Stress. She acknowledges that weight loss is principally concerned with dieting and exercise but adds chronic stress can play a significant role in weight gain. But even if yours derives from a noble place, it can nevertheless take years off your life. And that is not worth it – take it from the experts. It is certainly no way to achieve longevity. Besides, it merely adds weight, and in large chunks, at that. Food is a commonly utilized source of stress-relief, but ironically, it transforms into an obsession or coping mechanism that in turn ends up incurring more stress.

Ultimately, that is why Dr. Kellyann introduces several strategies for tackling the stress that may permeate your schedule or habits. What is more, these methods are intended for anyone regardless of their situation. But before exploring those stratagems, she doubles down on why chronic stress is a negative ether. Because chronically stressed bodies demand relief, and often, unfortunately, quick fixes do not generate substantial positive change. She then cites research that analyzes stress-eating, and the indications are staggering. These stress foods are generally the ones that are the worst for us, as they contain chemicals designed to scratch that itch, as it were. You must avoid them if you are to get anywhere in either weight loss or stress loss.

Next, stress makes you old and wrinkly, to put it bluntly. When stressed, the hormone cortisol is released and directly sends a lot of fat straight to the belly. When these cortisol levels remain at such a high level, this negatively impacts the blood glucose levels and growth hormones. No matter how young you are, it can give you a gut. Additionally, chronic stress weakens the collagen you produce, causing the skin to sag. And when you are stressed, it becomes more challenging to take care of yourself. An avalanche of self-destructive behaviors can materialize.

Thus, Dr. Kellyann offers five methods that can afford you the ability to cut stress out of your life. Although life can get busy, you must make time to cut the harmful stress out of your life. Even a little bit of an effort will go a long way, be it thirty or even five minutes. The first method involves meditation, something most people associate with gurus and hippies. But meditation can alter your brain, reclaim control over overeating behaviors, and slow your aging. It can also lower blood pressure, improve immune functions, and reduce anxiety and depression. And meditation is easy to utilize. Find a quiet place, get comfortable, concentrate on your feelings, connect with your surroundings, let your mind wander, and focus on breathing. Meditate for ten minutes a day, take small strides. You can even meditate while doing an activity. These can include taking a walk, cooking, and yardwork.

The second option involves different breathing techniques. Stress makes your breathing worse, harsher, and shallower. After a while, this can add up to a ton of damage to your body. The best way to tackle it head-on is by focusing on your present breathing. Like meditation, sit in a quiet place and comfortable position and focus on breathing. Once you become aware of your breathing, you can make it fuller. Your body will become more effective at releasing your stress into the universe. Lie on the floor, pause consistently to ponder your breathing techniques, and above all, learn to relax. She offers some easy-to-follow exercises that can help you harness your most relaxed self through breathing.

For the third option, Dr. Kellyann insists you get a massage. But first, stop viewing massages as a guilty pleasure, as they can be incredibly beneficial, and everyone deserves them in this stressful world. She cites research that backs up her claim even further. It is a medical treatment that can help keep you young and release stress through oxytocin. It is often worth the reasonable price that you can find it offered. She then introduces a meaningful segue into the power of love for yourself.

For option four, the doctor recommends going outside. She begins this section by asking you to picture yourself in your natural human condition, as a lion in the jungle would be in its natural environment. As a human, you would be a hunter and gatherer. Dr. Kellyann asks you to tap into this image, albeit a tad glorified. It is not to say that we should live in caves. It is to say that there is a fundamental connection between exercise and human prosperity. And tapping into that natural law could prove beneficial to your dieting efforts.

For the fifth option, Dr. Kellyann recommends laughter. While it may sound cliché, often the most cliché things ought to hold the most robust kernels of wisdom and truth. Laughing releases stress by enabling free blood flow to organs, relieving some of that amassed stress, and strengthening your immune defenses. Additionally, laughter burns calories, so you can lose your waistline while getting the most out of life at the same time. Even though these are small sacrifices, they are still positive actions that have tangible results on your stress. Who knows, you may walk away with a different attitude about life completely, and this may prove to be the most transformative of all.

Chapter Eleven

The last chapter suggests a slim mind to ensure that all this weight stays off for good. At the core of weight loss is an emotional component that too often goes unnoticed. And this stands in the way of success for many. As previously mentioned, emotions can play a role in overeating out of stress. No matter what serious event occurs in our lives, it is up to us to maintain good health to live a long and prosperous life. For some, this may involve avenues such as spirituality. Moreover, being in tune with dietary habits is, in a sense, spiritual. If you exist in an unhealthy mind frame or environment, it will likely produce the conditions for you to live an unhealthy life.

Thus, it is necessary to eliminate any poor dietary decisions and other toxic habits for broader personal growth. In this sense, the Bone Broth Diet is just as a mental and emotional commitment as it is physical. Ultimately, no matter how often you utilize the previously outlined tips for removing stress in your life, you must remove yourself from these structures that reproduce stress to make any serious headway.

Even something as simple as comparing yourself to the old version of yourself can trip you up and stall your weight loss. Those comparisons only weigh you down, and so you must leave them at the wayside. The good news is that if you believe in yourself, anything is possible. Just ask the countless people that Dr. Kellyann interviewed, whose lives changed through the Bone Broth Diet. By taking the first step and committing to 21 days, just one time could have profound, lasting effects on your view of everything you hold dear in life. Safety, love, importance, and motivation are all crucial components. You will need to harvest each of these ingredients in your garden, as it were.

Additionally, there are numerous ways to take the next big step towards a more peaceful mind. The first option is to choose your inner circle wisely. While this may not, at the outset, seem relevant, it indubitably is. The people who support your vision are worth keeping. In a sense, we are who we surround ourselves with, and Dr. Kellyann understands this to its atomic level. Her writing articulates the importance and possibility for anybody to implement positive steps towards keeping a non-toxic circle of friends and loved ones in their lives. But how can you tell if your inner circle is helping you prosper? Check to see if they leave you feeling energized, feeling better about yourself if they listen to you, and they hold you accountable.

Secondly, you must have an inner doorman. This step goes hand in hand with the previous one. The doorman within you must be comfortable with kicking people out who drain your energy while letting in the right people when it is fruitful for you to do so. It is their job to play this essential role of regulating the pathways to your joy. Do it, and you will effectively invest in your future tenfold. The people that reinforce your positive behaviors may be few — but quality, not quantity, matters.

Thirdly, you must strategize your yeses. What this means is you must not say yes to everything all the time. Doing so is exhausting and will set you back by inviting unnecessary stress and toxic people, environments, and situations. Be careful not to be manipulated for the goals and gains of others. For many people, they must learn the hard way — and this includes Dr. Kellyann. The humble writer goes into her experience with the subject, and the reality is most people go through this. It is a part of the human condition. But as humans, we must transcend and overcome even ourselves – and this means we must learn how to empower ourselves while being more honest with others as well about what we want and can do for them when asked to help. By saying yes less often, you can regulate a multitude of stressors and continue your metamorphosis.

For the fourth step, Dr. Kellyann urges breaking free from bad relationships. If you find yourself in an unhappy one, that is okay and normal. But it is time to change that instantly. Your future version of yourself will thank you greatly. That is because you will benefit immensely and immediately from taking care of yourself in this essential way. Bad relationships are toxic for you for numerous reasons. And while that may seem obvious, life happens. Bad relationships grow subtly, and so one must be vigilant, even if they do not find themselves in one presently. But how can you tell, you might ask. The doctor recommends a simple precaution: look at yourself in the mirror and analyze your skin, hair, and weight. Be honest with yourself. And if you feel yourself stressing at every turn, you must change this. An anecdote with a client is shared, and it is moving and lends itself to this lesson.

For the fifth step, Dr. Kellyann posits that you must live your truth, no matter what it may be. To deny yourself your identity is to deny yourself any chance of making your life better. By being in tune with who you have been, who you are, and who you will become, you can make tangible steps daily that will dramatically improve your mental, emotional, and physical health. That is why she integrates a brave analysis of the realities that women must address constantly surrounding their bodies. Women, she suggests, share a unique relationship to weight loss. And lying, the universal response to an inability or unwillingness to take life head-on, can prove too easy of an escape route from your problems. However, this can lead to drastic repercussions. By bottling up your emotions, you are effectively sabotaging yourself.

For the sixth step, you must learn the power of the word next. Life has segues and challenges, and you must take this head-on, even if these situations are terrifying. It is okay to admit that you are worried or scared. That is the first step to letting go of the power that fear has over you. By embracing the power of moving at a forward trajectory, you can get through the hardships that seem big now but will be eclipsed in comparison later down the road, when you have realized your personalized success. She cites one of her clients, Cheryl, and shares a heartfelt experience that demonstrates the power of this subtle superpower.

For the seventh step, Dr. Kellyann recommends letting someone else carry the emotional burdens required of others. You are not contractually obligated to capitulate to the emotions of others, no matter how big your heart is. You owe it to yourself to draw that boundary. When you feel stuck, you will turn to the negative outlets that are most familiar to you. That often translates to overeating foods that are terrible for you. By refusing to people-please, you will take considerable stress off your life.

Background Information About *Dr. Kellyann's Bone Broth Diet*

This book was published in 2015 and became a New York Times number one bestseller. It is part of the legacy that Dr. Kellyann has built over the years. And that legacy has helped hundreds of clients transform their bodies and lives. Readers can take that leap into the unknown and may find that it works for them as well. One only needs to input the Bone Broth Diet into a cursory search engine to find that many people have embarked on such journeys. Dr. Kellyann is tapping into that global, but especially Western and European demand for weight loss in the unconventional yet timeless way. All else aside, these are real people implementing the bone broth diet into their lives, and they are finding legitimate success with it for the most part.

Naturopathy is a legitimate branch of medicine. Indeed, there are accredited degree paths in its field. And Dr. Kellyann Petrucci has spent both under-graduate and post-graduate education learning both naturopathy and non-naturopathy. Naturopathic doctors get the same amount of training as other doctors. Kellyann is a perfectly credible source for dietary and nutritional information. If the rich and beautiful go to her, she must know her stuff, the reader assumes somewhat tongue-in-cheek. But reading through this cookbook and philosophy book, it is easy to become invested in the realities of the Bone Broth Diet.

Background Information About Dr. Kellyann Petrucci

First, J.J. Virgin wrote the forward. And it sets the tone nicely for the book. Virgin acknowledges the skepticism but insists that giving Dr. Kellyann's diet could prove to be a wise decision. It is hard not to agree. Virgin writes from a literary place of fervor and it is infectious to read how he too relates to the winds of change, how he too struggles with skepticism, and how he too witnesses a rising cultural shift in self-help and dieting. It is a solid introduction to the book, and it instantly captures the spirit of its contents.

Second, in terms of her credentials, Dr. Kellyann Petrucci has a Master of Science degree and is an accredited naturopathic doctor. As a writer, she has scored four New York Times bestselling books, including this one, Kellyann's Bone Broth Cookbook, The 10-Day Belly Slimdown, and Dr. Kellyann's Cleanse and Reset. In total, she has written six bestselling books, and her work has appeared in numerous top-rate journals such as The Wall Street Journal and Harper's Bazaar. In addition to her naturopathic and literary work, Petrucci hosts successful PBS specials like 21 Days to a Slimmer, Younger You.

Third, in her work as a concierge doctor for celebrities, she wields the benefits of her education. She holds the rare title of being one of the few Americans certified in biological medicine by the Switzerland doctor, Thomas Rau. Additionally, Petrucci has frequently appeared on such hit morning and daytime news programs such as *Dr. Oz* and *Good Morning America*. In her work, be it implicitly or explicitly, she frequently fights for recognition for naturopathy.

Trivia Questions

1. What does BDNF stand for?
2. True or false: The Bone Broth Diet avoids soy products.
3. True or false: sugar keeps you young.
4. True or false: you cook the bones to activate the most nutrients in the broth.
5. True or false: meditation is easy.

Discussion Questions

1. Why does Kellyann Petrucci consider exercise to be primal, and why does she suggest it in tandem with the Bone Broth Diet?
2. How does stress lead to weight gain?
3. How can mini fasting be advantageous for you? In what situations could it be dangerous for you?

More books from Smart Reads

Summary of The Case for Keto by Gary Taubes
Summary of Eat Smarter by Shawn Stevenson
Summary of 4 Hour Body by Tim Ferriss
Summary of Dr. Gundry's Diet Evolution by Dr. Steven
     Gundry
Summary of Exercised by David E. Lieberman
Summary of End Your Carb Confusion by Eric C. Westman
     with Amy Berger
Summary of Fast This Way by Dave Asprey

Thank You

Hope you've enjoyed your reading experience.

We here at Smart Reads will always strive to deliver to you the highest quality guides.

So I'd like to thank you for supporting us and reading until the very end.

Before you go, would you mind leaving us a review on Amazon?

It will mean a lot to us and support us creating high quality guides for you in the future.

Thanks once again!

Warmly yours,

The Smart Reads Team

Download Your Free Gift

As a way to say "Thank You" for being a fan of our series,
I've included a free gift for you:

Brain Health: How to Nurture and Nourish Your Brain For
Top Performance

Go to www.smart-reads.com to get your
FREE book.

The Smart Reads Team

Made in the USA
Columbia, SC
04 June 2021

39062094R00028